IF FC

MW01124778

Greater Than a Tourist Book Series
Reviews from Readers

I think the series is wonderful and beneficial for tourists to get information before visiting the city.

-Seckin Zumbul, Izmir Turkey

I am a world traveler who has read many trip guides but this one really made a difference for me. I would call it a heartfelt creation of a local guide expert instead of just a guide.

-Susy, Isla Holbox, Mexico

New to the area like me, this is a must have!

-Joe, Bloomington, USA

This is a good series that gets down to it when looking for things to do at your destination without having to read a novel for just a few ideas.

-Rachel, Monterey, USA

Good information to have to plan my trip to this destination.

-Pennie Farrell, Mexico

Great ideas for a port day.

-Mary Martin USA

Aptly titled, you won't just be a tourist after reading this book. You'll be greater than a tourist!

-Alan Warner, Grand Rapids, USA

Even though I only have three days to spend in San Miguel in an upcoming visit, I will use the author's suggestions to guide some of my time there. An easy read - with chapters named to guide me in directions I want to go.

-Robert Catapano, USA

Great insights from a local perspective! Useful information and a very good value!

-Sarah, USA

This series provides an in-depth experience through the eyes of a local. Reading these series will help you to travel the city in with confidence and it'll make your journey a unique one.

-Andrew Teoh, Ipoh, Malaysia

GREATER THAN A TOURIST- KOCHI KERALA INDIA

50 Travel Tips from a Local

Steffi George Manavalan

Cover designed by: Ivana Stamenkovic
Cover Image: https://pixabay.com/photos/kochi-india-kerala-backwaters-1644549/

CZYK Publishing Since 2011.

Greater Than a Tourist
Visit our website at www.GreaterThanaTourist.com

Lock Haven, PA
All rights reserved.
ISBN: 9781798494363

> TOURIST

50 TRAVEL TIPS FROM A LOCAL

BOOK DESCRIPTION

Are you excited about planning your next trip?

Do you want to try something new?

Would you like some guidance from a local?

If you answered yes to any of these questions, then this Greater Than a Tourist book is for you.

Most travel books tell you how to travel like a tourist. Although there is nothing wrong with that, as part of the Greater Than a Tourist series, this book will give you travel tips from someone who has lived at your next travel destination.

In these pages, you will discover advice that will help you throughout your stay. This book will not tell you exact addresses or store hours but instead will give you excitement and knowledge from a local that you may not find in other smaller print travel books.

Travel like a local. Slow down, stay in one place, and get to know the people and the culture. By the time you finish this book, you will be eager and prepared to travel to your next destination.

Inside this travel guide book you will find:

- Insider tips from a local.

- A bonus book *50 Things to Know About Packing Light for Travel* by bestselling author Manidipa Bhattacharyya.

- Packing and planning list.

- List of travel questions to ask yourself or others while traveling.

- A place to write your travel bucket list.

OUR STORY

Traveling is a passion of the "Greater than a Tourist" series creator. Lisa studied abroad in college, and for their honeymoon Lisa and her husband toured Europe. During her travels to Malta, an older man tried to give her some advice based on his own experience living on the island since he was a young boy. She was not sure if she should talk to the stranger but was interested in his advice. When traveling to some places she was wary to talk to locals because she was afraid that they weren't being genuine. Through her travels, Lisa learned how much locals had to share with tourists. Lisa created the *Greater Than a Tourist* book series to help connect people with locals. A topic that locals are very passionate about sharing.

TABLE OF CONTENTS

DEDICATION

This book is dedicated to my parents and husband who are from Kochi and the reason why my roots are so strong to this vibrant city.

ABOUT THE AUTHOR

Steffi is a Kochi-based writer with a penchant for travel. She is an ardent fan of good dessert and spicy food, and loves dreaming about all the fascinating places there are in the world, one day hoping to see them all. Her love story with Kochi goes a long way back into her childhood when she was raised within the walls of this phenomenal city.

HOW TO USE THIS BOOK

The *Greater Than a Tourist* book series was written by someone who has lived in an area for over three months. The goal of this book is to help travelers either dream or experience different locations by providing opinions from a local. The author has made suggestions based on their own experiences. Please do your own research before traveling to the area in case the suggested places are unavailable.

Travel Advisories: As a first step in planning any trip abroad, check the Travel Advisories for your intended destination.
https://travel.state.gov/content/travel/en/traveladvisories/traveladvisories.html

FROM THE PUBLISHER

Traveling can be one of the most important parts of a person's life. The anticipation and memories that you have are some of the best. As a publisher of the Greater Than a Tourist book series, as well as the popular *50 Things to Know* book series, we strive to help you learn about new places, spark your imagination, and inspire you. Wherever you are and whatever you do I wish you safe, fun, and inspiring travel.

Lisa Rusczyk Ed. D.
CZYK Publishing

WELCOME TO
> TOURIST

*"The world is a book and those
who do not travel, read only one
page."*

– Saint Augustine of Hippo

Namaste and welcome to the seaside gem of Kochi! This little area of about 400 square kilometers holds pieces of much that I am today. Also known as Cochin, this city's multi-cultural influences, historic towns, flavorsome food, world-class resorts and warm hospitality have given it the title of being one of the top tropical tourist destinations in the world.

Kochi is one of those unique cities that comprise of the welcome mix of having both a booming metro and a serene countryside within its ambit. Recently, honeymooners have been preferring the peaceful lagoons of Kochi, lined with coconut trees overlooking a brilliant orange sunset, for their first getaway together.

I hope this book will be an inspiration for you to travel more and explore the best of Kochi.

1. BEAT THE TROPICAL HEAT!

Kochi's intensely humid climate favors its green pastures and lush hillside cultivations. Usual day time temperatures range from 77-104°F. As the state of Kerala is near the equator, this tropical climate remains much the same with each season.

You will find yourself sweating profusely in the city's blistering heat. Packing light dresses, plenty of sunscreen and showering off the heat can quell those weather woes. Staying in shady areas and enjoying cooling drinks like coconut water can also be a welcome relief when exploring Kochi by foot.

2. BEST TIME TO VISIT KOCHI

The monsoons bless Kochi with heavy rain showers and thunder in the months of June to August. The inclement weather causes major tourist attractions such as waterfalls and trekking spots to close during these times. Knowing this after making all your books might be a damper literally also.

Which then is the best time to visit Kochi?

Any time between October to February is optimum! Good weather is just one of the few bonuses during this time – These months also revitalize the city with a series of lively festivals.

New Year celebrations are a big event in Fort Kochi where locals uphold the year-end tradition of burning a mammoth-sized Santa Claus amidst booming music and festivities. Year end is the peak season for Kerala tourism, which means the prices of hotels are on an all-time high during these months.

The month of September fares well for the budget-friendly traveller due to its lower accommodation prices. This is also the time for Onam throughout Kerala. Onam is a 10-day harvest festival that ushers in spending and vitality into the lives of locals in a flurry of celebratory events. Dances such as the puli kali (tiger-dance), chendamelam (musical drum performance) and flower shops begin to align the sides of the streets. Elaborate flower carpets are prepared in homes and corporate establishments, and a lavish 20+ dish meal is cooked up for lunch on the day of Thiruvonam. Consider visiting Kochi during this time as it offers some of the best sights of a city alive with culture, tradition and festivities.

The Onam festival changes its date every year, but usually takes place right after the monsoon season.

3. TACKLING BUS TRAVEL IN KOCHI

Kerala's official state buses are known as the "KSRTC" (Kerala State Road Transport Corporation) or "transport" buses. They ply along numerous routes connecting cities and towns and dock at localized KSTRC bus stands.

In Kochi, the most centralized bus stands are located at Kacheripady, Menaka and Vytilla. Depending on whether you want a superfast bus with limited stops or a regular one, the fare may vary. The air-conditioned orange buses, commonly known as the "AC Volvos" are super luxurious, offer safer and more comfortable travel. The red slightly smaller buses are privately owned and have a history of being in the hands of rash drivers.

Men usually sit at the back seats of the bus and women, at the front. I find that travelling during the rush hour between 7am-10am and 3pm-7pm is a daunting task! If ever you need help getting down at the right spot, you can ask the ticketmaster to tell you when your stop has reached.

4. TAKING AN UBER OR OLA CAB

Uber and Ola cabs are 2 good taxi services that run within Kochi city limits. They are safe for 24 hour travel and have fixed rates that ensure you are not being cheated. I have travelled in Uber multiple times and find that they are a good option for women travellers. And the fact that all you need is a mobile application to book a ride makes it even simpler to use!

5. TAKE THE WATER WAYS

You might not find any other city in India which has so many water bodies connecting to it. On the west, the Arabian Sea carpets out all the way to the Gulf shores. On the south, the serene Vembanad Lake glistens like jewels. All around the city are small rivers and ponds with quiet habitats surrounding them. This makes water transport an imminent mode of travel for locals. A few public water transportation options you can take advantage of are the:

- Vytilla to Kakkanad State Government ferry (saves several minutes of precious time as the roadway on this route has extremely bad traffic)
- Kochi to Varappuzha boats (has a stop at Kadamakkudy, a picturesque paddy field surrounded by coconut groves from where you can see some of the best sunsets in Kerala)
- High Court or Ernakulum Jetty to Fort Kochi ferry (the cheapest way to see the tourist-friendly Fort Kochi and Mattancherry)
- Kochi to Vypin ferry (Vypin is known for fresh seafood and the sprawling Vypin beach and lighthouse)

Private houseboats are a good option to explore the Vembanad Lake. But there is another cheaper way to see the same sights at a fraction of the cost. The government-owned tourist boat service from Kochi to Kollam and Alappuzha has an 8-hour ride through the calm waters of the lake, taking you through paddy fields, lotus farms and silent nostalgic villages. This boat ride shows you the place where the famous Nehru Boat Race takes place and allows a stop at the ashram of Matha Amrithanantha Mayi.

6. THE UMBRELLA AND CAP ARE YOUR BEST FRIENDS!

Kochi's hot and humid climate guarantees periodic and unexpected rain showers even in the scorching sunny daytime. Always carrying an umbrella with you wherever you go is often a prudent decision.

If you don't have an umbrella, you can easily buy one in any of the leather and shoe shops on the street. If an umbrella is not an option, you can also use disposable ponchos. In Kochi, these are more commonly known as raincoats and I use them all the time whenever heading out in light rain.

For day time use, bring a cap along to fight out those nasty UV rays! UV radiation is very strong in this part of the globe.

7. FORT KOCHI – WHERE IT ALL BEGAN

The history of discovering Kochi by Western civilization began at Fort Kochi, when the Portuguese established their first settlement within its streets. The area was then later populated by many sects of society – the French, Jews, English and the Dutch, who have all left their own distinct marks on the town's art and culture scene.

Some of the streets in Fort Kochi and Mattancherry still carry their European architectural accents. Fort Kochi and its surrounding areas are home to the marine wing of the Indian Navy which has established training centers and housing colonies on its streets. A rich trading dock has brought different sects from across India to this place as well. Traders from Gujarat, Rajasthan, Bengal and Maharashtra have private storage areas near the Vallarpadam and Fort Kochi ports. Generations of non-Keralite trading families have for decades intermingled with the local populace to create a harmonious and multi-faceted culture.

The fisheries business has been booming for centuries in this area. You will find creative cafes, artists, writers, spice merchants and boutique hotels along these streets. Fort Kochi also has amazing high-end restaurants serving flavorsome international cuisine.

A glimpse into Kochi's colonial past etched with modernity is what you can expect from this bustling artisan town.

8. DELVING THROUGH TIME AT THE KERALA FOLKLORE MUSEUM

There is something very rustic and even spiritual about stepping into the Kerala Folklore Museum in the naval town of Thevara. Containing over 5000 artifacts from three distinct cultures within Kerala (Malabar, Kochi and Travancore), this museum showcases sculptures, paintings, dance costumes, musical instruments, ritual items and masks excavated from numerous sites in the state. The museum itself is built in deeply traditional architecture and is a truly pleasant sight to see.

If you have the time, check out one of the classical dance performances or recitals at this museum. The loud booms of classical music resonating throughout the wood-lined theatre is an otherworldly experience altogether.

9. BEING COCONUTS ABOUT COCONUTS!

Perhaps the best part of Kochi is the ultra-hydrating tropical fruit – the coconut, and its availability at every nook and corner! The entire state of Kerala is famous for coconut production. You can see houses enveloped by curtains of coconut trees all over the streets of Kochi. If you are ever thirsty or feel like you could use a good pick-me-up drink in the midst of the blistering heat, head over to any of the coconut sellers by the roadside and ask for coconut water, colloquially known as, 'thengya vellam.' They will give you cool fresh coconut water straight out of the coconut itself!

The coconut industry has been constantly booming over the last decades with a steady export rate for coir products and organic oil.

Did you know that coconut is the most commonly used ingredient in Kerala cooking? If you are allergic to it, informing your hosts or waiter well before the food is prepared would save you from a great deal of trouble.

10. EATING WITH THE HAND – AND HEART!

You might be surprised at the table etiquettes practiced in Kochi during lunch and dinner time. Usually, people eat with their freshly-washed hands. Most restaurants place spoons, forks and knifes on the table, but for majority of the food, you might have to use your hands to be able to eat properly. This is extremely common when eating at the homes of hosts or with locals.

Eating with the hand is predominant throughout India as the scientific belief is that the food gets mixed thoroughly only when eaten with clean fingertips.

11. BEST FOODS TO TRY IN KOCHI

Where do I begin?! Kochi is a melting pot of flavors with its local favorite ingredients being fish, coconut oil and green chilly. This coastal heaven boasts of exquisite seafood, mostly caught fresh and cooked immediately.

Must-try foods of Kochi include the fried pearlspot, fish wrapped in banana leaf, tapioca and banana chips, Christmas plum cake and pickled mango and gooseberry. Two unique breakfast items you can find in any Kochi hotel or homestay is the rice flour-based puttu and nool appam (or string hoppers made from rice).

Your trip would be incomplete if you skip tasting the milk-rich dessert "payasam" served with an elaborate 20+ dish Kerala rice meal called the "Sadhya." The Kerala Sadhya is a meal typically served during lunch time at marriages and hotels, comprising of multiple servings of food on a large banana leaf. Rice, ghee, poppadum is accompanied by at least 7 curries of various textures in a rotating fashion. This complete meal balances different tastes, and though it may be extremely filling, has all the ingredients to fight stomach troubles caused to its invigorating tastes.

12. KEEP CALM AND HAVE SPICY FOOD

When in Kochi, you are bound to try some amazing local cuisine such as the fish wrapped in banana leaf, red fish curry, tapioca chips and other roast dishes. Almost 90% of Kochi food is extremely spicy. While making your order, specifically mention your spice preference.

Spicy food can also give you stomach troubles and that is a big damper to any vacation! Stocking up a few essential medicines to fight out such issues can be a life saver.

13. KOCHI FOR VEGANS AND VEGETARIANS

Vegetarians have awesome dining options in Kochi! The greatest meal of them all, the Kerala sadhya, available at almost every hotel, is 100% vegetarian. Dosa houses such as Pai Brothers, Indian Coffee House and BTH have fantastic vegetarian food for main courses, appetizers and snacks. Restaurant chains such as the Indian Coffee House and Saravana Bhavan have been ranked well across

South India for serving amazing vegan and vegetarian food that are light on the wallet.

A restaurant I love eating at when a vegetarian craving hits is the Dwaraka hotel on MG Road in Kochi city center. They consistently serve high quality food, worth the few extra rupees you pay, and have a sweet sambhar that is unmatched by any sambhar preparation anywhere else in Kerala. Desserts are made on a daily basis and they even give you milk with nutritional powders if you ask them.

Another good option for veg lovers are the many dhabas and Punjabi outlets across the city. Kochi has a widespread Punjabi population who have lent their distinct taste to the restaurant scene with their horde of mouthwatering dishes. Paneer or Indian cottage cheese is a commonly served item in their restaurants. This cheese comes in various combinations such as tikka masala, fry, scrambled, tandoori and smoked paneer cubes.

A quick FYI – plant-based milk is not easy to come by. Soy and almond milk is often pricey and can be found only in the largest supermarkets such as the LuLu Hypermarket at Edappally.

14. A PEEK INTO ROYALTY – PALACES IN KOCHI

History-rich Kochi hosted royal families for many centuries before and after western invasion. Their ancestral abodes have now been converted in heritage museums and renaissance palaces. If you are an ardent history buff, I suggest visiting the following palaces:

•   Hill Palace, Tripunithura – This former residence of the Maharaja of Cochin is a lavish white building surrounded by picturesque flower gardens, fountains and elegant courtyards. As the name suggests, the palace is located on top of a hill near the bustling city. The Hill Palace showcases the opulent lifestyle of the Maharajas by displaying their day-to-day used items such as crowns, swords, paintings, court artifacts and ancestral jewelry. You can easily spend 2-3 hours roaming about the well-maintained deer park on the palace premises, occasionally bumping into avid photographers trying to capture the natural beauty of the place.

•   Bolgatty Palace – This Dutch palace is a quaint mansion perched beside the Kochi International Marina. It was built with Dutch, English and Keralite architectural influences and has been converted into a full-scale heritage hotel with a convention center. The Bolgatty Palace has been much more commercialized than the Hill Palace.

•   Mattancherry Palace – For a palace that was built in 1555, the place holds an everlasting charm showcasing its brilliant construction style. The Mattancherry Palace was the home to several royal families and after western invasion, to the Dutch. The initial layout of the palace is in traditional Kerala style with labyrinths and lobbies lined with wooden planks. The Maharaja had set up a private temple for the Hindu Goddess Bhagvathi within the compound and had artisans create thousands of paintings and sculptures in praise of the deity.

15. LIFE'S A BEACH

The city lights of Kochi hang like a string of pearls on the shores of the Arabian Sea. Plenty of lagoons and beaches line its seaside. Two of my favorite places at hangout by the sea are at the Fort Kochi beach near the city center and the Cherai beach near Paravoor.

These two beaches have distinct personalities, with the former one being laden with rocks, heavily populated and lined with Chinese fishing nets; and the latter being quiet and secluded. The Fort Kochi beach draws crowds of all types – sand artists, kite flyers, football maniacs, fisher folk, writers and one-of-a-kind street food vendors. Cherai beach is famous for its fish food preparation. Live catches are cooked, sizzled and barbequed right before you and served with chilled drinks to cool your palette.

16. A NOTE ABOUT NOTES

Carrying cold hard cash notes of lower denominations such as Rs 10, 20, 50 and 100 is considered more practical than walking around with a credit card. Cash is more commonly accepted by small shops, for regular commute and at food stalls. Even taxi drivers (privately hired ones unlike Uber and Ola) often demand cash payment.

If you run out of cash at hand, there are ATMs at almost every kilometer mark within the city radius. You can ask your taxi driver to take you to one, or rely on Google Maps to spot the nearest ATM.

I have found many notes with numbers and names written on them. Please understand that these are invalid and you should neither give nor accept them. Same goes for torn, folded and heavily soiled notes.

17. MESSING WITH THE MOSQUITO!

Mosquitoes are ever-present miniature monsters that give both tourists and locals a hard time. You can avoid them by staying clear of water puddles, closing the doors and windows of your homestay or hostel at dusk and by using an effective mosquito repellant. Some brands of mosquito repellant for indoor use include Mortein, Good Knight and All Out. Odomos is another one which is easily available in medical stores in cream form so that you can apply it on-the-go.

You can also bring a good mosquito repellant from your home country.

18. GETTING CAUGHT IN A CHINESE FISHING NET!

The most photographed sight in Kochi is of the Chinese fishing nets that hang around the coasts of the city. These huge fishing nets have a unique method to catch fish and are operated by a team of 6 men. At certain places, they spread open to over 20 meters! That is a lot of fish they are going to get in there!

I think these Chinese nets make beautiful backdrops against the purple setting sky in photos. The nets also make up a part of the coastal architecture that show how Kochi has been influenced by other world cultures.

19. FOR THE NIGHT OWLS!

I find that travelling at night in Kochi is not safe for both men and women due to a number of reasons. Most often, late-night transportation is quite limited. Shops close between 7pm to 9 pm and alleyways become dark and lonely. Police patrol is present, however, may not always be on time.

Jot down the numbers of the nearest police station where you are staying and keep the official India police helpline number (just dial 100 from your phone) handy.

Being indoors by 10 pm is a good idea when travelling in Kochi.

20. WHAT TO SEE NEARBY

One of the best things about Kochi is that it is just 1-2 hours away from several amazing scenic locations. So if the city no longer entertains you, check out this list of renowned tourist places:

•   Kodanad Elephant Training Center and Sanctuary – This elephant sanctuary is 41 kilometers away from the city center and good for a day trip. Children can enjoy playing with baby elephants and watch them being washed and cleaned, an often fun and exhilarating experience for everyone including the elephant!

But if the thought of watching animals being chained upsets you, skip this visit. Elephants serve many purposes in Kerala, ranging from religious to domestic. People who look after them have a special place in society.

- Athirappilly and Vazhachal Waterfalls – These beautiful waterfalls have graced the sets of dozens of Indian films. The route that continues from Athirappilly to Sholayar Dam is known for seeing wildlife like the endangered hornbill (state bird of Kerala), bison, elephant, deer and rare snakes. Best time to visit the waterfalls would be during the rainy season when there is sufficient waterflow. You can club this visit with the Kodanad elephant sanctuary stop as they are nearby.

- Mararikulam Beach – This sandy beach is known for being relaxing and private with loads of exclusive docks and lagoons which you can explore at your own pace. It is located in Alappuzha district and is 50 kilometers away from Kochi. Mararikulam beach is surrounded by a range of 5-star resorts, organic fruit farms and lily ponds. I would call it a little drop of heaven on the Malabar coast.

Other places include the surreal tea plantations of Munnar, grassy hill tops of Wagamon (a hot paragliding spot!) and the Periyar Tiger Reserve, all which are more than 3 hours away from the city.

21. STAYING IN HERITAGE HOTELS

If you would like to experience Kerala tradition in the lap of luxury, I suggest staying at a heritage hotel. Kochi has converted many of its iconic palaces and homes to culturally rich yet modern housing abodes for the opulent traveller. Such hotels have rooms built in traditional wooden decor that open into private backwaters, courtyards and gardens. They allow the guest to experience the well-preserved culture of a decade gone by in an atmosphere with world-class amenities.

Heritage hotels in Kochi can be found mainly on the sea-facing areas of Fort Kochi, Marine Drive and Bolgatty. These hotels usually have ayurvedic centers attached to them and offer international cuisine along with Kerala food.

22. WARM WATER VS. COLD WATER

As a general practice, restaurants and hotels serve warm water instead of chilled. Sometimes, this water maybe flavored with cumin or herbs. Such water comes in a pale yellow or slight pink color. If you would like cold water, you will have to specifically request it at most hotels.

23. BEST STREET FOOD IN KOCHI

Did you know that Kochi has a large population of Bengalis (people from the state of West Bengal) who whip up just the best street food? My all-time favorite North Indian snack food is the stuffed triangular samosa. Chicken puff pastry comes second in the list. These are 2 must-try street foods in Kochi that are available practically everywhere!

Street sellers also roast peanuts and wrap them up in little paper cones for just a couple of rupees. The Kulukki sarbath is another hit street drink that is dear and near to every Keralite's heart. Essentially, this is a version of shaken and stirred lemonade, topped with basil seeds, pineapple and sometimes, even green chilly.

You can also find many street vendors selling cut fruits rubbed with chilly powder and salt. Eat these at your own discretion after examining the surroundings and method of storage.

At 4 pm, when offices have their tea breaks, street sides being to smell heavenly with different types of snacks starting to align sidewalks. Another one of my favorite tea time snacks is the pazhampori or banana fritters (bananas deep fried in a coating of gram and all-purpose flour). Then, there is bonda (gram flour dumplings stuffed with potatoes), sukhiyan (gram flour balls stuffed with cooked peas and coconut), parippuva (deep fried spicy lentil cakes), kumbilappam (coconut and jaggery steamed in a ball of rice flour and wrapped in a banana leaf) and uzhnnu vada (fluffy deep-fried lentil rings).

Just describing these delicious snacks me drool!

24. WHERE TO GO TO BUY GROCERIES

I always go to the nearest neighborhood family-owned grocery markets for the freshest produce. These are usually small shops with low prices that change daily. If you are stringent about having organic food, there are a couple of organic vegetable shops located in Kaloor. Supermarkets such as Bismi, Reliance Fresh, Margin Free, More, SupplyCo and Grand Fresh are bigger in size and stock up on more processed products like cereals, white bread, jams and cookies. LuLu Mall has a huge hypermart on its first floor that has even rare fruits such as dragon fruit and artichokes. You can also find imported products such as toilet paper, certain nuts and dry fruits at this hypermart.

25. AWAKEN YOUR SENSES WITH AYURVEDA

I am sure many of you visiting Kochi would be eager to try one of the most famous offerings of the state – Ayurveda. Kerala is the home of Ayurveda and Kochi has a fair share of establishments that practice this medicinal technique responsibility.

This rejuvenating therapy is a herbal healing technique for various types of ailments. I have felt that ayurvedic body massages are very relieving as during the treatment, the muscles loosen up to release all the stress locked up in them and become fresh. Ayurvedic stomach cleansing and skin disease treatments are recommended world-wide, and if you are in the home of Ayurveda, why not give it a try?

A quick FYI - Make sure you specify to your therapist if you have any allergies before beginning any sort of treatment.

26. AT HOME ON A HOUSEBOAT

Kochi is surrounded by thousands of waterways, rivers and rivulets, coursing in every direction between homes and connecting islands. Houseboats or kettuvallams traverse through these emerald waterways, showing both tourists and locals the beauty of Kerala from the waterline.

Houseboats are large covered wooden boats designed to accommodate a kitchen, living room, restroom and bedrooms. These leisure boats have facilities similar to hotels, come with chefs onboard and guarantee privacy so that you can enjoy floating through the waterways of Kochi on your own or with good company.

Routes that houseboats usually ply on are the main ones across the Vembanad Lake connecting Kochi to Kollam district. You cannot do the entire route in one day due to its length, but just parts of it - yes! Gliding along the water gives you sights that only few have seen – like the quiet riverside village life treading past quickly, sprawling lotus farms, blooming paddy fields and glorious sunsets.

Whenever possible, ask for photos of your boat before booking and if possible, inspect it personally before finalizing your trip.

27. DINING WITH THE LOCALS

If you truly want to experience Kochi food and hospitality, you can choose to dine in people's homes. There are organized programs through which you can meet locals who offer to share a hearty Kerala meal with you right in the center of their homes. You can expect the warmth of a gracious host, taste of lip-smacking food and bouts of experience-sharing common when two parties from different sides of the world meet.

What is even better is that some of them will even arrange for interesting activities to do before and after the meal. This is a very real way to become a part of the lives of a Kochi local.

28. WHEN YOU MISS WESTERN FOOD!

Did you know that you are not that far away from home after all? At least gastronomically! When you are craving western food, prepare to be surprised by the huge variety of fast food options to satiate your hunger pangs! There is Pizza Hut, Subway, Dominos, KFC, Costa Coffee and many more global chains that have established base in Kochi. Some of them are in shopping malls such as the Lulu or Central Mall. The others you can find on MG Road and towards places near the city center.

Interestingly, these brands have localized additions to their menus. But the classics remain the same. So goodbye spicy food and hello crispy fried chicken! What a welcome relief right?

29. WE ALL SCREAM 'ICE CREAM!'

A go-to dessert I have at any time of the day whenever I go out is ice cream! Ice cream shops have boomed in Kochi over the last few years with all types of parlors opening bases here. There are places that sell natural flavored ice creams where you can taste the raw fibrous strands of mango and jackfruit. Italian gelatos and custard-based treats are also now available in plenty throughout the city.

If you miss your home town ice cream, I have just the right fix for you – head over to a branch of Coldstone Creamery or Baskin Robbins and scoop into one of their indulgent frozen treats. Everything will feel much better after having ice cream!

30. BEING PREPARED FOR BANDHS AND HARTHALS

Perhaps one of the downsides of life in the state of Kerala is the frequency of harthals and bandhs. These are protests by political unions for various causes and result in a total shutdown of transport and commercial services. You will not find much private transport and risk being in the pathway of the protest if venturing out. Shops will remain closed at least till 6pm, offices and schools will not open and most public services such as banks and tourism offices come to a standstill.

Generating awareness on the dates of such protests by following newspapers with English editions, such as the Malayala Manorama will keep you one step ahead of others when a bandh or harthal is announced.

31. IN THE HEART OF FESTIVITIES IN KOCHI

Kochi's culture is a mix of art, modernity and seaside tradition. This fabric facilitates for the right mix of people who come together to create enjoyable festivals and events for those of diverse interests.

41

The Kochi-Muziris Biennale is an international art festival that occurs in Fort Kochi every 2 years. The highly successful turnout of the festival has brought dozens of creative artists from around the world to the city.

Another hugely popular festival is the Cochin Carnival, a New Year special parade that takes place again on the streets of Fort Kochi. This event is a celebration of music and eclectic dance and ends in the burning of a Santa Claus effigy amidst fireworks. Thousands of LED installations, fireworks and special lighting effects illuminate the streets of Fort Kochi during this last week of December, making it a must-go party destination for New Years.

Onam season in Kochi is one of my favorite times to be in city because of the mad rush of harvest festivities. It is also the single biggest shopping time in Kerala due to the wide range of discounts you get on electronics, clothes and gifts.

32. THE SHOPPER'S PARADISE – BROADWAY AND MG ROAD

The best shopping deals in Kochi city can be found on a street named "Broadway." This is my go-to place to shop for shoes, accessories, textiles and even to eat some good masala dosas! The sellers out here deal more in wholesale items. Footwear, handbags, suitcases, tailoring services, copper and silver utensils and decor items have amazing bargain prices here. What stands out about this street is that it is very crowded, but if you venture inside enough, you will get merchandise at super low prices – a tip for budget travellers!

MG Road or Mahatma Gandhi Road is another road famous for shopping. All the big brands – Levi's, Lee Cooper, Hidesign, Clarks, Adidas, Van Heusen, Skechers, Baskin Robbins, The Body Shop – are all right here. If you are looking for traditional Kerala attire, I feel shopping at the larger textile shops like Seematti, Jayalakshmi and Kalyan Silks will get you good quality products at the standard market prices.

33. CATCH A KATHAKALI PERFORMANCE

The Kalamandalam Vijayan Kerala Kathakali Center in Kochi showcases the folk art of kathakali to locals and tourists in its authentic form and setting. This famous theatre has been featured on BBC, National Geographic and other international channels for being the one of the very few places left in India that host this beautiful art.

Be ready to be wowed by not just kathakali, but other traditional art forms as well such as bharathanatyam, kutchipudi and mohiniyattam. Carnatic and Hindustani musical performances also take place on different days of the week.

Recently, the center began to hold yoga and meditation classes as well for people of all ages.

You will have to make reservations in advance to see any of the art shows.

34. ACCESS TO PUBLIC RESTROOMS

This is a tricky part when it comes to travelling in Kochi. Public restrooms are hard to come by and it is always best to carry some toilet paper and hand sanitizer with you when using them. Your safest bet is to finish up all your businesses at the places you stop for food or visit any of the large shopping malls where bathrooms are clean, neat and free.

35. GUEST ETIQUETTE

If you have made some local friends during your Kochi trip, there is a good chance that they might have invited you home for lunch or dinner. I know the fears people have when coming over for the first time, especially when you are in a new country. These are some techniques I regularly practice to calm my nerves when going over to people's homes for the first time, and I hope they help you too:

• Bringing a gift – Always bring a little gift for the family who has invited you. Edible items such as dry fruits, sweets, cakes and chocolates are always welcomed. Alcohol is usually avoided when gifting.

• Removing shoes – Leaving your shoes outside when entering the home shows great respect for your friend's property.

• Asking for cold water and cutlery – It is okay to ask for spoons and forks to eat your food. Most households know that eating with hands is not common outside south Asia, and chances are that they have already accounted for this.

- Managing spice level – If you find the food too spicy for your tastes, mix in more rice with a smaller quantity of the curry. If it gets too overwhelming, you can always politely tell your host that the food was too hot. They will definitely understand.

- Being on time – Dinner time is usually between 8 pm to 10 pm, and lunch between 12 pm to 2 pm in most Kerala households. When visiting, plan to come according to this time frame.

- Be prepared to be surprised – Chances are that most households will be super excited to have a foreigner with them and they might overwhelm you with lots of food, photos and questions. Guest is God for us in Kochi and you will mostly get godly treatment when you are in their homes.

- Topics of contention – Just so you know, delving too much on certain topics can at times tip the comfort meter, especially if there is any alcohol on the table. Opinionating on topics such communist ideologies, politics and religious beliefs during the first visit can backfire sometimes.

36. WEARING COTTON AND A SENSE OF DRESSING

In the humid climate of Kochi, cotton clothes with breathable layers are most comfortable. Sandals and flip flops are best recommended for ease of walking. You are expected to remove footwear before entering worship buildings.

Many places in Kochi are conservative in their approach towards women wearing shorts and showing too much skin. The Kerala saree or set mundu and jubba and mundu are two local dressing styles that you must try while in Kochi! You can even ask people to help you out in wearing at local beauty parlors or at your homestay.

37. STREET ART IN FORT KOCHI

Searching for some Instagram-worthy street art spots? Fort Kochi is the best place to see street art in Kochi. Art painted by established artists to smaller creative drawings by locals can be found across the

Aspin Wall, walls of the Pepper House and on certain streets such as the Burger street.

During the Kochi-Muziris Biennale, the amount of street art decorating Fort Kochi increases tenfold. You will also notice that some artworks are alive with satire and comedy, while others have an out-of-the-world visual appeal.

38. LOCAL CRAFTS BY COMMUNITIES IN KOCHI

Local crafts made in Kochi include products carved out of coir, coconut, tusks, animal horns, bamboo and different types of wood. These native ingredients are processed and toughened to create mats, masks, bags, footwear, decor pieces and spice boxes. Bell metal items such as oil lamps, utensils and bowls are both durable and decorative in nature.

A common decor item you can see in houses in Kochi is a wooden carving of an elephant or a long boat. These two icons are synonymous with Kerala culture and lifestyle.

Textile is another area where the Kochi artisans have proven their mastery. Pure silk or 'kasavu' is a rich natural fiber made from silkworms. They adorn dresses, bags, shoes, head gear and even artificial jewelry. Silk sarees are a major business in Kochi. The 6 meters of flawless textile is an object of pride and attraction for women in Kochi.

Durbar Hall in South Kochi has period exhibitions where vendors come to sell their crafts. You can walk into these usually free exhibitions at any time to check out the plethora of items made by their artisans.

In case you forget to purchase craft items or are unable to carry them with you to your home country, you can always order them online through the state government's official retailer on Amazon.

39. AQUA TOURISM AT MATSYFED AND KUMBALANGI INTEGRATED TOURISM VILLAGE

Do you know what this seaside city is most famous for? There is a clue right in the question! - Fish of course!

Kochi is a central haven for the fisheries business due to its favorable state policies and excellent water levels. For years, a substantial source of income for the city was from selling fish and fish products. This is also the reason why you find high quality seafood in Kochi, while not in the eastern districts of the state.

Both salt and fresh water fishes are available in plenty throughout Kochi. If you ever want to get to know the fisheries business a bit more in detail, visit the Matsyafed Aqua Tourism Fish Farm in either Malipuram or Njarackal. This fish farm comprises of a huge area dedicated to cultivating fish. The natural beauty of its habitats has been brilliantly preserved and you can explore its scenic lagoons by manned boats. If you are lucky, you can also catch flying fish falling right into your boat!

Day programs include a lavish seafood lunch with fried squid, shark, pearlspot, shrimp and other types of fish, private paddle boating and rest areas with hammocks to unwind after a hearty meal.

If you prefer to be within the city limits, I suggest visiting the Kumbalangi Integrated Tourism Village. Here, you can get to interact with paddy cultivators, farmers, toddy workers and fisher folk who make a living in the area. You can also book private country boat through coconut groves or sunset cruises with delicious seafood dinners.

40. DRIVING RULES AND SAFETY

You might not drive much when you are on a short vacation. However, just a few guidelines in case you decide to get behind the wheel.

In India, the driver sits on the right side. All cars come with a 'clutch.' Automatic gears are not very common. Seat belts are compulsory only for the driver and extra children's seats are not available over the counter. The maximum number of people on a motorbike is two and the helmet is mandatory only for the driver. Unless specifically mentioned with a sign board, all roads are two-way.

The following documents are mandatory to have with you at all times – driving license, vehicle registration certificate, insurance, taxation and fitness certificates.

You might be alarmed by the number of pedestrians crossing the road without using the zebra crossing. It is a bit of a challenge I admit to drive in Kerala when you are unfamiliar with crowded roads and cities.

41. REAL LIFE VS. REEL LIFE

People in Kerala take their film stars very seriously. If you ever have trouble beginning a conversation with someone from Kerala, just ask them if they like 'Mammootty' or 'Mohanlal' more. The words will flow out of their lips faster than lightning!

Movies usually release every Friday and you can see large masses of people swarming movie theatres on this day. Kochi city is also the home to many Malayalam movie stars with some of the top names in the industry owning house and apartments within the city limits.

42. ALCOHOL AND CIGARETTE USE

Kochi is known for having many 5-star and 4-star bar that are open 24/7. There are also regular bars with crowds that are more local. However, pubbing is not a very predominant phenomenon within the city.

You can purchase all types of alcohol at liquor stores such as Bevco, ConsumerFed Foreign Liquors and Kerala State Beverages Corporation outlets, but cannot consume it in public venues. And yes, that applies to beer and wine too!

The state government has also banned smoking cigarettes in designated areas with 'No Smoking' signs. Usually, smoking within closed environments, hotels and public places is not allowed.

43. WHY LOCALS LOVE MARINE DRIVE

One of the secret spots I would visit when bunking classes during my college days was Marine Drive. Every person in Kochi has had some sort of association with this place. And if you pay it a visit, you will too.

Marine Drive is a charming seaside walkway giving fantastic views of the city and the sunset. This hotspot is a hit with people of all ages who come here to catch some fresh air, jog, meet friends and sample some street food.

The lighted Rainbow Bridge on the walkway looks spellbindingly beautiful at night. You can also take boat tours from this spot to Fort Kochi, Vypin and other places.

Best thing of all - the strip is entirely free to enter and is close enough to public transport, great restaurants and shopping malls.

44. FOR THOSE ON THE SPIRITUAL PATH

Religion has always played a big role in the life of Kochi residents. Temples, shrines, churches and graveyards associated with spiritual beliefs have been erected everywhere. Visiting these iconic places can give you a greater idea of their historic significance in the daily life routines of people in Kochi:

• St. Francis Church, Fort Kochi – This church is one of the first European churches in India established when the Portuguese discovered the Kochi coast in the 15th century. It held the remains of Portuguese explorer Vasco da Gama for a brief period and has an empty tomb in memory of the local residents who died in World War I. The Dutch, Portuguese and British influences can be seen on its architecture.

• Paradesi Synagogue – The Mattancherry Jewish Synagogue in Jew Town is one of the only remaining synagogues in use by the Jewish community of Kochi. This historic synagogue houses several rare gifts, inscriptions and scrolls presented by noteworthy Jews, rulers and religious figures to the Jewish community of Kochi.

- Chottanikkara Bhagvathi Temple – Hindu devotees flock to this temple to pray to the supreme Goddess Bhagvathi for her blessings. Located within the city limits, the temple sits in the sacred town of Chottanikkara, a place known for its vast Hindu believer community.

- Sree Mahadeva Temple at Aluva Manappuram – This temple rises to utmost glory on the day of Shiva Rathri, a colorful celebration for deceased ancestors, occurring in February or March on the banks of the Periyar river. Devotees from across Kerala flock in thousands to this temple to place offerings in a huge event which involves massive traffic regulations and sometimes even gives way to declaring government holidays. The temple is also subject to high levels of flooding every year.

- Jain Temple – The Jain Temple of Mattancherry was built in the 15th century for the worship of Jains from Gujarat and Rajasthan. An event that takes place exclusively at this Jain Temple is the pigeon feeding. Every day at noon, the higher authorities of the temple spread many kilograms of grain on their courtyard to feed pigeons. The happy birds have been fed this way for over 25 years.

45. DON'T BE FOOLED BY THOSE WAGGING TAILS

Stray dogs that roam around the alleyways, owner-less and drooling, pose a real threat to anyone passing by. Such dogs are untamed, often have diseases and can attack without any provocation. There have been unfortunate reports of children dying from stray dog attacks. I strongly suggest using caution when around strays and by no means should you feed them.

46. NEWSPAPERS AND ONLINE MEDIA

The best way to find know about current happenings in Kochi is to purchase English daily newspapers such as the Hindu or the Indian Express. These are 2 newspapers I trust to give accurate news about local happenings. Their regional editions also provide detailed information about city events, possible road closures and changed public transport timings. You can also follow their websites and social media accounts for updates.

47. VISITING THE LAKSHADWEEP ISLANDS

The Lakshadweep Islands are a set of 36 islands around 200 kilometers off the Kochi coast. Exclusive transportation to these islands either by flight, chopper, cruise and boat, is available only from Kochi in Kerala.

These rich atoll lands are scenic isles full of coconut groves and coral reefs. The local population has a unique self-dependent lifestyle based on coir manufacturing and fishing.

What attracts tourists most to these islands is the presence of certified scuba diving agencies, glass bottom boat rides and water sports. Some of the highest concentrations of corals, turtles and coastal birds in India are found in the Lakshadweep area. The land here is heavily protected by environment agencies, who have done their best to preserve the natural beaches and the life-giving blue waters.

Kochi is the only place in Kerala that offers connection to these islands. If you ever plan to visit this island paradise and you are in Kochi, then you are at the right spot!

48. BEST SOUVENIRS FOR FRIENDS BACK HOME

Getting back to friends and family with pieces of your trip doubles the joy for everybody! Some unique items you can pick up from Kochi as souvenirs and return gifts are freshly packed spices (cardamom, pepper, nutmeg, cinnamon, dry chilly, turmeric), handmade miniature models of elephants, boats, ornament boxes, coir products (bags, slippers, wall decor) and even textiles made from silk, such as the Kerala saree and mundu.

Another item available in the souvenir shops of Kochi is the Aranmula Kannadi, a special mirror made by polishing a metal plate with a particular ratio of copper and lead. Its manufacturing details are a well-kept secret among a few select families. Each mirror is handmade in an elaborate process by a dexterous craftsman. No two Aranmula mirrors are alike due to this human factor.

Jute is a versatile material that has been used extensively in manufacturing products such as bags, dresses, earrings and even footwear. You can consider buying jute items as souvenirs as well.

With so many options to choose from, your bags will definitely be full by the time you return home!

49. TAKING HOME A BIT OF KERALA COOKING!

It is not just things you can take home with you; you can also pride yourself in learning and mastering some quick and easy Kerala dishes in the kitchens of home chefs in Kochi. These days, due to the boom of interest in south Indian cooking worldwide, homemakers and restaurateurs offer cooking classes to tourists. They share recipes and tips on making unique Keralite dishes such as fish molly, fried pearlspot in banana leaves, puttu, vegetable stew, prawns roast and banana fritters.

What better way to end a vacation than by taking some fond tastes with you from new shores!

50. TRAVEL TO THE AIRPORT

CIAL or Cochin International Airport Limited is the nearest and most convenient airport for those staying in Kochi city. Private cabs and apps like Uber do provide rides to airport, but the best way to get there is by the orange KSRTC state-owned buses that depart from Fort Kochi every 30-45 minutes. This is a super cheap option especially if you do not have a lot of bulky baggage. You can board this bus from any major bus stop along its city route. The destination "Nedumbassery" or "CIAL" or "Airport" will be written at the front of the bus to inform possible passengers on the way.

TOP REASONS TO BOOK THIS TRIP

Heritage: Kochi is one of the oldest cities in India with a colonial past. Culturally, Kochi houses artists, craftsmen, dancers and musical maestros that have lent an everlasting touch to the fabric of Indian history. Historic palaces rich with architectural splendor are found at many places around the city.

Food: Undoubtedly, the king of Kerala cuisine resides here. In Kochi, you can get all sorts of cuisines cooked in various styles – international, local, fusion, street, savory… It is also a fantastic place to learn traditional cooking and sample a good mix up of regional specialties.

Connectivity: Kochi connects many districts together, making it a good spot to stay at while exploring other parts of Kerala. It is close to the international airport and other breathtaking tourist locations as well.

BONUS BOOK

50 THINGS TO KNOW ABOUT PACKING LIGHT FOR TRAVEL

PACK THE RIGHT WAY EVERY TIME

AUTHOR: MANIDIPA BHATTACHARYYA

Edited by Melanie Howthorne

ABOUT THE AUTHOR

Manidipa Bhattacharyya is a creative writer and editor, with an education in English literature and Linguistics. After working in the IT industry for seven long years she decided to call it quits and follow her heart instead. Manidipa has been ghost writing, editing, proof reading and doing secondary research services for many story tellers and article writers for about three years. She stays in Kolkata, India with her husband and a busy two year old. In her own time Manidipa enjoys travelling, photography and writing flash fiction.

Manidipa believes in travelling light and never carries anything that she couldn't haul herself on a trip. However, travelling with her child changed the scenario. She seemed to carry the entire world with her for the baby on the first two trips. But good sense prevailed and she is again working her way to becoming a light traveler, this time with a kid.

INTRODUCTION

*He who would travel happily
must travel light.*

-Antoine de Saint-Exupéry

Travel takes you to different places from seas and
mountains to deserts and much more. In your travels
you get to interact with different people and their
cultures. You will, however, enjoy the sights and
interact positively with these new people even more,
if you are travelling light.

When you travel light your mind can be free from
worry about your belongings. You do not have to
spend precious vacation time waiting for your
luggage to arrive after a long flight. There is be no
chance of your bags going missing and the best part is
that you need not pay a fee for checked baggage.

People who have mastered this art of packing light
will root for you to take only one carry-on, wherever
you go. However, many people can find it really hard
to pack light. More so if you are travelling with
children. Differentiating between "must have" and
"just in case" items is the starting point. There will be
ample shopping avenues at your destination which are
just waiting to be explored.

This book will show you 'packing' in a new 'light' – pun intended – and help you to embrace light packing practices for all of your future travels.

Off to packing!

DEDICATION

I dedicate this book to all the travel buffs that I know, who have given me great insights into the contents of their backpacks.

THE RIGHT TRAVEL GEAR

1. CHOOSE YOUR TRAVEL GEAR CAREFULLY

While selecting your travel gear, pick items that are light weight, durable and most importantly, easy to carry. There are cases with wheels so you can drag them along – these are usually on the heavy side because of the trolley. Alternatively a backpack that you can carry comfortably on your back, or even a duffel bag that you can carry easily by hand or sling across your body are also great options. Whatever you choose, one thing to keep in mind is that the luggage itself should not weigh a ton, this will give you the flexibility to bring along one extra pair of shoes if you so desire.

2. CARRY THE MINIMUM NUMBER OF BAGS

Selecting light weight luggage is not everything. You need to restrict the number of bags you carry as well. One carry-on size bag is ideal for light travel. Most carriers allow one cabin baggage plus one purse, handbag or camera bag as long as it slides under the seat in front. So technically, you can carry two items of luggage without checking them in.

3. PACK ONE EXTRA BAG

Always pack one extra empty bag along with your essential items. This could be a very light weight duffel bag or even a sturdy tote bag which takes up minimal space. In the event that you end up buying a lot of souvenirs, you already have a handy bag to stuff all that into and do not have to spend time hunting for an appropriate bag.

I'm very strict with my packing and have everything in its right place. I never change a rule. I hardly use anything in the hotel room. I wheel my own wardrobe in and that's it.

Charlie Watts

CLOTHES & ACCESSORIES

4. PLAN AHEAD

Figure out in advance what you plan to do on your trip. That will help you to pick that one dress you need for the occasion. If you are going to attend a wedding then you have to carry formal wear. If not, you can ditch the gown for something lighter that will be comfortable during long walks or on the beach.

5. WEAR THAT JACKET

Remember that wearing items will not add extra luggage for your air travel. So wear that bulky jacket that you plan to carry for your trip. This saves space and can also help keep you warm during the chilly flight.

6. MIX AND MATCH

Carry clothes that can be interchangeably used to reinvent your look. Find one top that goes well with a couple of pairs of pants or skirts. Use tops, shirts and jackets wisely along with other accessories like a scarf or a stole to create a new look.

7. CHOOSE YOUR FABRIC WISELY

Stuffing clothes in cramped bags definitely takes its toll which results in wrinkles. It is best to carry wrinkle free, synthetic clothes or merino tops. This will eliminate the need for that small iron you usually bring along.

8. DITCH CLOTHES PACK UNDERWEAR

Pack more underwear and socks. These are the things that will give you a fresh feel even if you do not get a chance to wear fresh clothes. Moreover these are easy to wash and can be dried inside the hotel room itself.

9. CHOOSE DARK OVER LIGHT

While picking your clothes choose dark coloured ones. They are easy to colour coordinate and can last longer before needing a wash. Accidental food spills and dirt from the road are less visible on darker clothes.

10. WEAR YOUR JEANS

Take only one pair of Jeans with you, which you should wear on the flight. Remember to pick a pair that can be worn for sightseeing trips and is equally eloquent for dinner. You can add variety by adding light weight cargoes and chinos.

11. CARRY SMART ACCESSORIES

The right accessory can give you a fresh look even with the same old dress. An intelligent neck-piece, a couple of bright scarves, stoles or a sarong can be used in a number of ways to add variety to your clothing. These light weight beauties can double up as a nursing cover, a light blanket, beach wear, a modesty cover for visiting places of worship, and also makes for an enthralling game of peek-a-boo.

12. LEARN TO FOLD YOUR GARMENTS

Seasoned travellers all swear by rolling their clothes for compact and wrinkle free packing. Bundle packing, where you roll the clothes around a central object as if tying it up, is also a popular method of compact and wrinkle free packing. Stacking folded clothes one on top of another is a big no-no as it makes creases extreme and they are difficult to get rid of without ironing.

13. WASH YOUR DIRTY LAUNDRY

One of the ways to avoid carrying loads of clothes is to wash the clothes you carry. At some places you might get to use the laundry services or a Laundromat but if you are in a pinch, best solution is to wash them yourself. If that is the plan then carrying quick drying clothes is highly recommended, which most often also happen to be the wrinkle free variety.

14. LEAVE THOSE TOWELS BEHIND

Regular towels take up a lot of space, are heavy and take ages to dry out. If you are staying at hotels they will provide you with towels anyway. If you are travelling to a remote place, where the availability of towels look doubtful, carry a light weight travel towel of viscose material to do the job.

15. USE A COMPRESSION BAG

Compression bags are getting lots of recommendation now days from regular travellers. These are useful for saving space in your luggage when you have to pack bulky dresses. While packing for the return trip, get help from the hotel staff to arrange a vacuum cleaner.

FOOTWEAR

16. PUT ON YOUR HIKING BOOTS

If you have plans to go hiking or trekking during your trip, you will need those bulky hiking boots. The best way to carry them is to wear them on flight to save space and luggage weight. You can remove the boots once inside and be comfortable in your socks.

17. PICKING THE RIGHT SHOES

Shoes are often the bulkiest items, along with being the dainty if you are a female. They need care and take up a lot of space in your luggage. It is advisable therefore to pick shoes very carefully. If you plan to do a lot of walking and site seeing, then wearing a pair of comfortable walking shoes are a must. For more formal occasions you can carry durable, light weight flats which will not take up much space.

18. STUFF SHOES

If you happen to pack a pair of shoes, ensure you utilize their hollow insides. Tuck small items like rolled up socks or belts to save space. They will also be easy to find.

TOILETRIES

19. STASHING TOILETRIES

Carry only absolute necessities. Airline rules dictate that for one carry-on bag, liquids and gels must be in 3.4 ounce (100ml) bottles or less, and must be packed in a one quart zip-lock bag. If you are planning to stay in a hotel, the basic things will be provided for you. It's best is to buy the rest from the local market at your destination.

20. TAKE ALONG TAMPONS

Tampons are a hard to find item in a lot of countries. Figure out how many you need and pack accordingly. For longer stays you can buy them online and have them delivered to where you are staying.

21. GET PAMPERED BEFORE YOU TRAVEL

Some avid travellers suggest getting a pedicure and manicure just the day before travelling. This not only gives you a well kept look, you also save the trouble of packing nail polish. Remember, every little bit of weight reduced adds up.

ELECTRONICS

22. LUGGING ALONG ELECTRONICS

Electronics have a large role to play in our lives today. Most of us cannot imagine our lives away from our phones, laptops or tablets. However while travelling, one must consider the amount of weight these electronics add to our luggage. Thankfully smart phones come along with all the essentials tools like a camera, email access, picture editing tools and more. They are smart to the point of eliminating the need to carry multiple gadgets. Choose a smart phone that suits all your requirements and travel with the world in your palms or pocket.

23. REDUCE THE NUMBER OF CHARGERS

If you do travel with multiple electronic devices, you will have to bear the additional burden of carrying all their chargers too. Check if a single charger can be used for multiple devices. You might also consider investing in a pocket charger. These small devices support multiple devices while keeping you charged on the go.

24. TRAVEL FRIENDLY APPS

Along with smart phones come numerous apps, which are immensely helpful in our travels. You name it and you have an app for it at hand – take pictures, sharing with friends and family, torch to light dark roads, maps, checking flight/train times, find hotels and many other things. Use these smart alternatives to traditional items like books to eliminate weight and save space.

I get ideas about what's essential when packing my suitcase.

-Diane von Furstenberg

TRAVELLING WITH KIDS

25. BRING ALONG THE STROLLER

Kids might enjoy walking for a while but they soon tire out and a stroller is the just the right thing for them to rest in while you continue your tour. Strollers also double duty as a luggage carrier and shopping bag holder. Remember to pick a light weight, easy to handle brand of stroller. Better yet, find out in advance if you can rent a stroller at your destination.

26. BRING ONLY ENOUGH DIAPERS FOR YOUR TRIP

Diapers take up a lot of space and add to the weight of your luggage. Therefore it is advisable to carry just enough diapers to last through the trip and a few for afterwards, till you buy fresh stock at your destination. Unless of course you are travelling to a really remote area, in which case you have no choice but to carry the load. Otherwise diapers are something you will find pretty easily.

27. TAKE ONLY A COUPLE OF TOYS

Children are easily attracted by new things in their environment. While travelling they will find numerous 'new' objects to scrutinize and play with. Packing just one favorite toy is enough, or if there is no favorite toy leave out all of them in favor of stories or imaginary games.

28. CARRY KID FRIENDLY SNACKS

Create a small snack counter in your bag to store away quick bites for those sudden hunger pangs. Depending on the child's age this could include chocolates, raisins, dry fruits, granola bars or biscuits. Also keep a bottle of water handy for your little one.

These things do not add much weight and can be adjusted in a handbag or knapsack.

29. GAMES TO CARRY

Create some travel specific, imaginary games if you have slightly grown up children, like spot the attractions. Keep a coloring book and colors handy for in-flight or hotel time. Apps on your smart phone can keep the children engaged with cartoons and story books. Older children are often entertained by games available on phones or tablets. This cuts the weight of luggage down while keeping the kids entertained.

30. LET THE KIDS CARRY THEIR LOAD

A good thing is to start early sharing of responsibilities. Let your child pick a bag of his or her choice and pack it themselves. Keep tabs on what they are stuffing in their bags by asking if they will be using that item on the trip. It could start out being just an entertainment bag initially but with growing years they will learn to sort the useful from the superfluous. Children as little as four can maneuver a small trolley suitcase like a pro- their experience in pull along toys credit. If you are worried that you may be pulling it for them, you may want to start with a backpack.

31. DECIDE ON LOCATION FOR CHILDREN TO SLEEP

While on a trip you might not always get a crib at your destination, and carrying one will make life all the more difficult. Instead call ahead to see if there are any cribs or roll out beds for children. You may even put blankets on the floor. Weave them a story about camping and they will gladly sleep without any trouble.

32. GET BABY PRODUCTS DELIVERED AT YOUR DESTINATION

If you are absolutely paranoid about not getting your favourite variety of diaper or brand of baby food, check out online stores like amazon.com for services in your destination city. You can buy things online ahead of your travel and get them delivered to your hotel upon arrival.

33. FEEDING NEEDS OF YOUR INFANTS

If you are travelling with a breastfed infant, you save the trouble of carrying bottles and bottle sanitization kits. For special food, or medications, you may need to call ahead to make sure you have a refrigerator where you are staying.

34. FEEDING NEEDS OF YOUR TODDLER

With the progression from infancy to toddler, their dietary requirements too evolve. You will have to pack some snacks for travelling time. Fresh fruits and vegetables can be purchased at your destination. Most of the cities you travel to in whichever part of the world, will have baby food products and formulas, available at the local drug-store or the supermarket.

35. PICKING CLOTHES FOR YOUR BABY

Contrary to popular belief, babies can do without many changes of clothes. At the most pack 2 outfits per day. Pack mix and match type clothes for your little one as well. Pick things which are comfortable to wear and quick to dry.

36. SELECTING SHOES FOR YOUR BABY

Like outfits, kids can make do with two pairs of comfortable shoes. If you can get some water resistant shoes it will be best. To expedite drying wet shoes, you can stuff newspaper in them then wrap

them with newspaper and leave them to dry
overnight.

37. KEEP ONE CHANGE OF CLOTHES HANDY

Travelling with kids can be tricky. Keep a change of
clothes for the kids and mum handy in your purse or
tote bag. This takes a bit of space in your hand
luggage but comes extremely handy in case there are
any accidents or spills.

38. LEAVE BEHIND BABY ACCESSORIES

Baby accessories like their bed, bath tub, car seat, crib
etc. should be left at home. Many hotels provide a
crib on request, while car seats can be borrowed from
friends or rented. Babies can be given a bath in the
hotel sink or even in the adult bath tub with a little bit
of water. If you bring a few bath toys, they can be
used in the bath, pool, and out of water. They can also
be sanitized easily in the sink.

39. CARRY A SMALL LOAD OF PLASTIC BAGS

With children around there are chances of a number
of soiled clothes and diapers. These plastic bags help
to sort the dirt from the clean inside your big bag.

These are very light weight and come in handy to other carry stuff as well at times.

PACK WITH A PURPOSE

40. PACKING FOR BUSINESS TRIPS

One neutral-colored suit should suffice. It can be paired with different shirts, ties and accessories for different occasions. One pair of black suit pants could be worn with a matching jacket for the office or with a snazzy top for dinner.

41. PACKING FOR A CRUISE

Most cruises have formal dinners, and that formal dress usually takes up a lot of space. However you might find a tuxedo to rent. For women, a short black dress with multiple accessory options will do the trick.

42. PACKING FOR A LONG TRIP OVER DIFFERENT CLIMATES

The secret packing mantra for travel over multiple climates is layering. Layering traps air around your body creating insulation against the cold. The same light t-shirt that is comfortable in a warmer climate can be the innermost layer in a colder climate.

REDUCE SOME MORE WEIGHT

43. LEAVE PRECIOUS THINGS AT HOME

Things that you would hate to lose or get damaged leave them at home. Precious jewelry, expensive gadgets or dresses, could be anything. You will not require these on your trip. Leave them at home and spare the load on your mind.

44. SEND SOUVENIRS BY MAIL

If you have spent all your money on purchasing souvenirs, carrying them back in the same bag that you brought along would be difficult. Either pack everything in another bag and check it in the airport or get everything shipped to your home. Use an international carrier for a secure transit, but this could be more expensive than the checking fees at the airport.

45. AVOID CARRYING BOOKS

Books equal to weight. There are many reading apps which you can download on your smart phone or tab.

Plus there are gadgets like Kindle and Nook that are thinner and lighter alternatives to your regular book.

CHECK, GET, SET, CHECK AGAIN

46. STRATEGIZE BEFORE PACKING

Create a travel list and prepare all that you think you need to carry along. Keep everything on your bed or floor before packing and then think through once again – do I really need that? Any item that meets this question can be avoided. Remove whatever you don't really need and pack the rest.

47. TEST YOUR LUGGAGE

Once you have fully packed for the trip take a test trip with your luggage. Take your bags and go to town for window shopping for an hour. If you enjoy your hour long trip it is good to go, if not, go home and reduce the load some more. Repeat this test till you hit the right weight.

48. ADD A ROLL OF DUCT TAPE

You might wonder why, when this book has been talking about reducing stuff, we're suddenly asking you to pack something totally unusual. This is because when you have limited supplies, duct tape is immensely helpful for small repairs – a broken bag, leaking zip-lock bag, broken sunglasses, you name it and duct tape can fix it, temporarily.

49. LIST OF ESSENTIAL ITEMS

Even though the emphasis is on packing light, there are things which have to be carried for any trip. Here is our list of essentials:

• Passport/Visa or any other ID

• Any other paper work that might be required on a trip like permits, hotel reservation confirmations etc.

• Medicines – all your prescription medicines and emergency kit, especially if you are travelling with children

• Medical or vaccination records

• Money in foreign currency if travelling to a different country

• Tickets- Email or Message them to your phone

50. MAKE THE MOST OF YOUR TRIP

Wherever you are going, whatever you hope to do we encourage you to embrace it whole-heartedly. Take in the scenery, the culture and above all, enjoy your time away from home.

On a long journey even a straw weighs heavy.

-Spanish Proverb

PACKING AND PLANNING TIPS

A Week before Leaving

- Arrange for someone to take care of pets and water plants.

- Stop mail and newspaper.

- Notify Credit Card companies where you are going.

- Change your thermostat settings.

- Car inspected, oil is changed, and tires have the correct pressure.

- Passports and photo identification is up to date.

- Pay bills.

- Copy important items and download travel Apps.

- Start collecting small bills for tips.

Right Before Leaving

- Clean out refrigerator.

- Empty garbage cans.

- Lock windows.

- Make sure you have the proper identification with you.

- Bring cash for tips.

- Remember travel documents.

- Lock door behind you.

- Remember wallet.

- Unplug items in house and pack chargers.

READ OTHER
GREATER THAN A TOURIST
BOOKS

Greater Than a Tourist San Miguel de Allende Guanajuato Mexico:
50 Travel Tips from a Local by Tom Peterson

Greater Than a Tourist – Lake George Area New York USA:
50 Travel Tips from a Local by Janine Hirschklau

Greater Than a Tourist – Monterey California United States:
50 Travel Tips from a Local by Katie Begley

Greater Than a Tourist – Chanai Crete Greece:
50 Travel Tips from a Local by Dimitra Papagrigoraki

Greater Than a Tourist – The Garden Route Western Cape Province
South Africa: 50 Travel Tips from a Local by Li-Anne McGregor van
Aardt

Greater Than a Tourist – Sevilla Andalusia Spain:
50 Travel Tips from a Local by Gabi Gazon

Greater Than a Tourist – Kota Bharu Kelantan Malaysia:
50 Travel Tips from a Local by Aditi Shukla

Children's Book: Charlie the Cavalier Travels the World by Lisa
Rusczyk

>TOURIST

> TOURIST

Visit *Greater Than a Tourist* for Free Travel Tips
http://GreaterThanATourist.com

Sign up for the *Greater Than a Tourist* Newsletter for discount days, new books, and travel information:
http://eepurl.com/cxspyf

Follow us on Facebook for tips, images, and ideas:
https://www.facebook.com/GreaterThanATourist

Follow us on Pinterest for travel tips and ideas:
http://pinterest.com/GreaterThanATourist

Follow us on Instagram for beautiful travel images:
http://Instagram.com/GreaterThanATourist

> TOURIST

At *Greater Than a Tourist*, we love to share travel tips with you. How did we do? What guidance do you have for how we can give you better advice for your next trip? Please send your feedback to GreaterThanaTourist@gmail.com as we continue to improve the series. We appreciate your constructive feedback. Thank you.

METRIC CONVERSIONS

TEMPERATURE

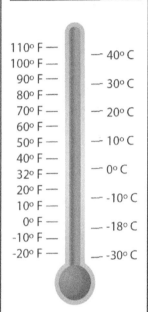

110° F — — 40° C
100° F —
90° F — — 30° C
80° F —
70° F — — 20° C
60° F —
50° F — — 10° C
40° F —
32° F — — 0° C
20° F —
10° F — — -10° C
0° F — — -18° C
-10° F —
-20° F — — -30° C

To convert F to C:

Subtract 32, and then multiply by 5/9 or .5555.

To Convert C to F:

Multiply by 1.8 and then add 32.

32F = 0C

LIQUID VOLUME

To Convert:................Multiply by
U.S. Gallons to Liters............... 3.8
U.S. Liters to Gallons 26
Imperial Gallons to U.S. Gallons 1.2
Imperial Gallons to Liters....... 4.55
Liters to Imperial Gallons 22
1 Liter = .26 U.S. Gallon
1 U.S. Gallon = 3.8 Liters

DISTANCE

To convert ....Multiply by
Inches to Centimeters 2.54
Centimeters to Inches 39
Feet to Meters...................... .3
Meters to Feet 3.28
Yards to Meters 91
Meters to Yards 1.09
Miles to Kilometers 1.61
Kilometers to Miles............ .62
1 Mile = 1.6 km
1 km = .62 Miles

WEIGHT

1 Ounce = .28 Grams
1 Pound = .4555 Kilograms
1 Gram = .04 Ounce
1 Kilogram = 2.2 Pounds

TRAVEL QUESTIONS

- Do you bring presents home to family or friends after a vacation?

- Do you get motion sick?

- Do you have a favorite billboard?

- Do you know what to do if there is a flat tire?

- Do you like a sun roof open?

- Do you like to eat in the car?

- Do you like to wear sun glasses in the car?

- Do you like toppings on your ice cream?

- Do you use public bathrooms?

- Did you bring your cell phone and does it have power?

- Do you have a form of identification with you?

- Have you ever been pulled over by a cop?

- Have you ever given money to a stranger on a road trip?

- Have you ever taken a road trip with animals?

- Have you ever went on a vacation alone?

- Have you ever run out of gas?

- If you could move to any place in the world, where would it be?

- If you could travel anywhere in the world, where would you travel?

- If you could travel in any vehicle, which one would it be?

- If you had three things to wish for from a magic genie, what would they be?

- If you have a driver's license, how many times did it take you to pass the test?

- What are you the most afraid of on vacation?

- What do you want to get away from the most when you are on vacation?

- What foods smells bad to you?

- What item do you bring on ever trip with you away from home?

- What makes you sleepy?

- What song would you love to hear on the radio when you're cruising on the highway?

- What travel job would you want the least?

- What will you miss most while you are away from home?

- What is something you always wanted to try?

- What is the best road side attraction that you ever saw?

- What is the farthest distance you ever biked?

- What is the farthest distance you ever walked?

- What is the weirdest thing you needed to buy while on vacation?

- What is your favorite candy?

- What is your favorite color car?

- What is your favorite family vacation?

- What is your favorite food?

- What is your favorite gas station drink or food?

- What is your favorite license plate design?

- What is your favorite restaurant?

- What is your favorite smell?

- What is your favorite song?

- What is your favorite sound that nature makes?

- What is your favorite thing to bring home from a vacation?

- What is your favorite vacation with friends?

- What is your favorite way to relax?

- Where is the farthest place you ever traveled in a car?

- Where is the farthest place you ever went North, South, East and West?

- Where is your favorite place in the world?

- Who is your favorite singer?

- Who taught you how to drive?

- Who will you miss the most while you are away?

- Who if the first person you will contact when you get to your destination?

- Who brought you on your first vacation?

- Who likes to travel the most in your life?

- Would you rather be hot or cold?

- Would you rather drive above, below, or at the speed limited?

- Would you rather drive on a highway or a back road?

- Would you rather go on a train or a boat?

- Would you rather go to the beach or the woods?

TRAVEL BUCKET LIST

1.

2.

3.

4.

5.

6.

7.

8.

9.

10.

NOTES

Made in the USA
Coppell, TX
21 December 2024

43237703R00069